A MIDNIGHT MOON

A MIDNIGHT MOON

r.h. Sin

Andrews McMeel
PUBLISHING®

A MIDNIGHT MOON

Andrews McMeel Publishing
a division of Andrews McMeel Universal
1130 Walnut Street, Kansas City, Missouri 64106

www.andrewsmcmeel.com

24 25 26 27 28 TEN 10 9 8 7 6 5 4 3 2 1

ISBN: 978-1-5248-8924-1

Library of Congress Control Number: 2023946529

Editor: Patty Rice
Art Director: Diane Marsh
Production Editor: Elizabeth A. Garcia
Production Manager: Shona Burns

ATTENTION: SCHOOLS AND BUSINESSES
Andrews McMeel books are available at quantity discounts with bulk purchase for educational, business, or sales promotional use. For information, please e-mail the Andrews McMeel Publishing Special Sales Department: sales@amuniversal.com.

INTRODUCTION

There's a lot going on with you, and even though a lot of things have changed over the past year, a lot of it still feels the same. You made commitments to yourself that are becoming more challenging to uphold. You've been through a lot, but you've managed to keep it together, and right now you're wondering how much longer you'll be able to withstand everything that's preventing you from finding peace.

I won't pretend to know all of your day-to-day challenges, and I can't even begin to fathom what you're really going through, but I can tell you this much: Behind every curtain, there lies a beautiful scene waiting to be discovered. After the storm has passed, you will find that there is an honest assortment of tranquility residing beyond the borders and that happiness is waiting for you there.

Wait just a tad bit longer, and you will be where you are meant to be, and you will experience the emotions that you are deserving of feeling. Please don't leave just yet.

THE GREAT ALONE

Here I am, surrounded by a sea of people, yet I
feel as if I'm the only one standing in this desolate
wasteland of emptiness, present in my own pain and
sorrow while smiling just enough to keep others from
realizing that something is wrong. The noise of the
crowd echoes in my ears, drowning out the sound of
my own thoughts. It's like being in a bubble, where
the world moves around you, yet you stand still.

I see them all laughing and talking, but I can't
connect with them. It's like I'm trapped in my own
world, my own misery. My loneliness is suffocating,
and I feel like I'm drowning in a sea of despair.
I'm screaming for help, but no one can hear me.
Screaming behind the silent smile laced with tears.

The sadness of feeling alone in the middle of a crowd
is a feeling that cannot be put into words. It's like
being lost in a maze with no way out. It's like being
trapped in a nightmare; no matter how hard you try,
you can't escape. Sometimes, I wonder if anyone will
ever understand the pain that I feel. The pain of being
isolated in a world that is so interconnected.

I stand here, in the middle of this crowd, feeling the
weight of my sadness pressing down on me. And I
wonder if anyone else has ever felt this way. If anyone
else has ever felt so alone, even when people surround
them. But there are moments, while sitting in the
thick of it all, when I believe that there is someone
in this crowd who feels the same way that I do, and
maybe that someone is reading this right now.

Sadness has always been a strange and powerful force in my life. A strange, tough, but profound friend of mine that still embodies a stranger. As a child, I was drawn to the melancholic melodies of music, finding solace in the way they reflected the sorrow I carried within. And, as I grew older, that sadness became a driving force in my creativity, propelling me to express myself in ways I never thought possible. The sadness, shadow life, has always fallen behind me, connecting itself to my feet, walking with me into every artistic meeting with my mind.

It's funny, really, how something so painful can be so transformative. How the weight of sadness can forge strength and resilience within us, shaping us into the people we were meant to be. For me, that strength came in the form of poetry, music, and cinema.

My creative output was born out of the depths of my sadness, a raw and unfiltered expression of the emotions I couldn't put into words growing up. Or maybe I just never felt that I had a voice to say what I really needed to say in the first place. And through poetry, I found a way to connect with others, to bring light to the darkness that surrounded us all.

But even in the midst of my joy, the sadness never truly went away. It lingers as a constant companion, reminding me of the fragility of life and the fleeting nature of happiness. And yet, it was that very sadness that gave my words their power, their ability to move and inspire.

Looking back on it all, I realize now that the power of sadness lies not in its ability to break us but in its capacity to transform us. We are forged in its fire, created new. To take the pain and suffering, we endure and turn it into something beautiful, something that can touch the hearts and souls of others. Just like these words are touching you in a profound way right now.

For me, that transformation was both a blessing and a curse, both a form of light and darkness all at once; it's like that moment when you notice the moon sitting in the sky along with the sun. It gave me a voice, a platform to speak out against what and who wanted to destroy me and to shed light on the struggles of those who felt unheard. But it also takes a toll, leaving me exhausted and emotionally drained.

Still, I wouldn't have it any other way. The power of sadness has shaped me in ways I never thought possible, teaching me the value of vulnerability and the importance of connection. And, even now, as I look back on my life and the impact my poetry has had, I'm grateful for every moment of sadness and pain, for they have made me who I am today.

So, to anyone who may be struggling with sadness, know that you are not alone. Know that there is strength and beauty to be found in the darkness and that your pain can be transformed into something powerful and inspiring. And always remember that, in the midst of even the most profound sadness, there is hope for peacefulness in your soul. I hope you figure out a way to cultivate whatever it is you need to survive those cold nights.

Having your heart ripped apart by the one you trusted most is a vicious blow. It's like pouring your soul out onto the pavement and watching as it gets trampled by intentionally uncaring feet. The pain is deep; it's a pit that you can't climb out of. You feel like a fool for ever letting them in, but you also feel like a fool for not being able to keep them. It's a terrible thing, but, in the end, you learn to live with it. You learn to be more cautious with who you let into your life, and you learn to be stronger, because you have no other choice but to be the greatest version of yourself, displaying characteristics that even you didn't believe you embodied.

Trusting the wrong people is a mistake that can haunt you for a lifetime. It's like picking up a snake without paying attention, thinking it's a rope, only to get bitten in the end. Toxic relationships are like that too; they lure you in with promises of love and care only to leave you bruised and battered. The ugliness of it all is hard to comprehend; it's like staring into the abyss and seeing your own reflection, only parts of yourself rendered unrecognizable. These people don't care about you; they only care about what they can get from you. They take and take and take until there's nothing left. It's a brutal game, and the only way to win is to walk away. The only way to be triumphant is to move forward without them.

In this modern era of screens and distractions, it's a daunting task to compete with someone's phone for their attention. It's as if the phone has become an extension of their very being, an inseparable limb that never leaves their side. The pings and buzzes of notifications are like a siren's call, luring them away from the present moment and into the abyss of digital temptation, a profound and meaningful war waged upon every present moment but a fight that so many are not willing to win. As I reflect on this phenomenon, I can't help but feel a sense of melancholy wash over me. Is this what our world has come to? Have we become so enamored with technology and overly attached to our devices that we've forgotten the simple pleasures of human connection? It's a heartbreaking realization, looking over at someone you love while they look into a screen that feels nothing for them.

––––––––––––––––––

I cannot help but be drawn to the topic of self-deception when it comes to relationships. It is as if we are in a constant battle with ourselves, trying to convince ourselves that our partner is worth the pain and suffering they cause us. We tell ourselves that they will change, that they love us deep down, that we cannot do any better. We cling to the illusion of a perfect relationship, even when it is clear that it does not exist. We look for the good in the worst of places, attempting to wash clean something that will always remain a mess. We are afraid of being alone, of not being loved, of not being enough. But, in reality, we are just lying to ourselves. We must face the truth that these toxic relationships are not worth the sacrifice of our own happiness, peace of mind, and overall well-being. Only when we let go of these lies can we begin to heal and move toward a better, more fulfilling life. And I want that for you. I want that for me. I want that for us all.

Let us begin the work of letting go; let us begin the difficult task of telling the truth to ourselves.

It is a cruel irony that those who claim to love us are often the ones who hurt us the most. Discovering that someone you love has been lying to you is a gut-wrenching experience. It plagues the soul like a sickness that feels impossible to get rid of. It feels like the ground beneath you is shaking, and you cannot trust anything you thought you knew. Your very belief in this person becomes a sham, like a religion with false idols. It is a betrayal of the deepest kind, and it leaves you feeling violated and exposed. And yet, these same people have the nerve to come to you, begging for forgiveness, as if their words could somehow make the pain disappear. Offering up a slew of empty apologies, only given in the time that their dirty deeds have been discovered. They act as if their remorse somehow erases the fact that they deliberately deceived you and that they actively chose to hide the truth from you. It is a blatant disregard for the trust and love you bestowed upon them, and it is a wound that can never fully heal. No amount of apologies can make up for the damage they have done, and, in the end, you are faced with the decision of staying or walking toward freedom and peace. I hope you discover the thing inside your heart that allows you to leave for good.

––––––––––––––––––

A person who masters the art of silently letting go is a person who is truly free. There is freedom in every step that leads you away from the person who has decided to break your heart.

---

i sit alone
sitting mid center
of a crowd

cold in a room
full of warmth
silent among
the chatter

observing what i'll never be
sad and yet happy
about what i can't become

———————————

I hope I lose everything not meant to stay in my life.
In a way, honestly, I hope you're one of those things.

———————————————

Trusting someone with your heart is a vulnerable act; unfortunately, it can sometimes lead to a nightmarish adventure. When you trust the wrong person with your heart, you open yourself up to the possibility of betrayal, heartbreak, and disappointment. This person may take advantage of your trust, use you for their own gain, or simply be unable to reciprocate the same level of feelings you have for them. It can be a painful experience to realize that someone you trusted and cared for has let you down, and it can take time to heal from the wounds that they may have caused. This experience is a teacher; inside of it all is a lesson, a harsh one. It's important to remember that not everyone is deserving of your trust and your heart and that it's ultimately up to you to take care of yourself and choose who you allow into your life. It is this misadventure that takes you down a road of everything you'll soon realize that you must avoid in order to reach the destination of your dreams. It is in the aftermath of the pain that you discover which road to take and what to ignore on the way.

Loneliness is a barren wasteland, a desolate place, a haunting and dreary scene where the echoes of your own heartache reverberate endlessly. It is the feeling of being trapped in a room full of people yet feeling as if you are the only one there, feeling like a ghost within a body that has become a shell of the place that used to feel like home. It is the ache in your chest that never seems to subside, the weight on your shoulders that feels insurmountable. A thought that keeps you restless when all you want to do is sleep. When you love the wrong person, loneliness takes on a whole new meaning. It is the realization that the one you love does not reciprocate your feelings, that they are a mirage in the desert of your heart. It is the knowledge that the person you crave will never give you the affection that you need, that they will always be out of reach. Sitting beside you but distant. Standing beside you but always present elsewhere.

It is a cruel and vicious cycle, this love for the wrong person. You pour your heart and soul into someone who will never see you as anything more than a passing moment, a fleeting thought. A resource for only a moment when they are in need. You cling to the hope that, maybe, just maybe, they will come to love you in the way that you love them. But it is a false hope, a dream that will never come to fruition.

Loneliness seeps into your bones, aching and gnawing at your insides. It is the knowledge that you are not enough, that no matter how much you give, it will never be enough to make them stay. It is the understanding that you are alone in your love, that it will never be returned in the way that you need.

In the end, loneliness becomes a part of you, an ever-present companion in your heart. A friend that you're ashamed of. It is a reminder of the love that could have been, the hope that was once there. It is a bitter pill to swallow, a reminder that sometimes love is not enough, that sometimes the person you love will never love you back.

But in the darkness of loneliness, there is also a glimmer of hope. It is the knowledge that you are strong enough to survive, that you are enough on your own. It is the understanding that love will come again, that there is someone out there who will love you in the way that you deserve. And in that hope, there is the possibility of a new love, a love that will fill the emptiness in your heart and make the loneliness disappear for a while, but I don't think you should wait there in your misery, because you will discover that your needs can be met by everything you hold within yourself.

A MIDNIGHT MOON

i fell in love with a narcissist
an attractive devil in disguise
with sparkling eyes and romantic offerings

i knew not of your soullessness
nor of your ego's towering height
i saw what i needed
even though it was never there

but soon enough I felt the pain
of your endless self-absorption

a reminder that the only thing
you cared for was yourself, devoted to your desire
to take without giving

you never saw my hidden depths
nor cared to know my heart
you only saw your own reflection
as we both stood before the mirror

i tried leaving
poured all my resources
into breaking free, but your hold on me
the strongest chains, built to imprison titans

now i stand here, wiser still, with scars
and lessons learned, and i know that love
is not a game
nor a prize to be earned

i found the strength to walk away
to heal and start anew
took awhile to understand
that i'm the one i must pursue

You notice bit by bit that something is wrong, but you ignore it because you never want to believe that the enemy is so close that they've become a friend hiding their intent to destroy whatever hope you have of being happy. The devil never looks the way you imagine, and hell isn't as hot as you believed. The evil is gradual; the unkindness is patient as it slithers into your life, silent as a garden snake, and only transforms into a serpent when it is too late.

---

from the beginning
some are born to bear a melancholic weight
a sadness that comes knocking
on their lives' doors like an unwelcome fate

their spirits bruise with ease
causing a disconnect that results
in a fall—like autumn leaves

painful gravity, the tears descend too fast
as if from a waterfall that never runs dry or past
the memories linger, haunt and cling
and pain endures like a song that hurts to sing

i see you because
i, too, am of this kind
alive in a nightmare
where peace is hard to find

the weight i bear
feels heavy as lead
as i run frantically through life
with a heart that's easily bled

but in my sorrow
i find a kind of grace
a sensitivity to life that others
often misplace

and though i may tire
and bruise with ease

i also see the beauty
that lies hidden beneath a winter's breeze

I purged every wasteful thought to make room for
more of what will grant me the opportunity to be at
peace whenever I think. I purged my life of all the
people who no longer deserved my presence just
so that I could make more room for the things and
people who encouraged my heart to feel the right
things. I purged the noise from my days and the static
that used to fill my nights just so that I could be more
present beneath the sun and rest easily beneath the
moon. There is a reward in the removal of what no
longer fits into one's life. There is a prize to be gained
when you decide to walk away from your abusers.

---

goodbye to the faded parts of my soul
goodbye to the broken heart that you've known
goodbye to the sadness that you caused
goodbye to this idea that we could evolve

goodbye to a future
one we'll never know
goodbye to these flowers
that died and wouldn't grow

goodbye to us
where memories fade
goodbye to the seconds
the minutes, the days

goodbye to the fights
stuck in our ways
goodbye to the ship
that's been sunk by the waves

goodbye to the tragedy
that we had become
goodbye to the light
goodbye to the sun

goodbye to the ways
that you played with my heart
goodbye is the end
so something better can start

goodbye to the good
that i once saw in you
goodbye to this idea
that you're the best
i could do

walking down a one-way street
in the wrong direction
entering a room filled with hate
expecting love

is there any truth
in your lies
i'm searching for a reason
to believe in something
that isn't honest

looking to be saved
by the person
who hurts me

the cure can't be found
in the reason for the sickness
and still, i look to you
while you focus on someone else

searching for
the right type of love
in the wrong person
is madness

can we be lonely together
sit in silence as we heal
quiet beneath a moon
that knows exactly how we feel

in the moment of pitch dark
can we discover each other's light
it doesn't need to be forever
but could you promise me
this night

can we be lonely together
you pick a time
show me a place

where rainstorms
are showers
a flood
where we can bathe

dirtied by my past
my heart just needs
to cleanse
or be somewhere with someone
where something new can begin

can we be lonely together
find solace in the present
the way to mend a broken heart
is to search it for a lesson

we can learn from the cracks
there is strength in the sadness
there is power in what is broken
there is beauty in the madness

can we be lonely together
you decide when you're ready
you don't have to face this on your own
i'll be here if you let me

Surrounded by many but alone inside herself.

_____

In love alone; wrong person by my side.

Chasing after shadows, realizing the light was within me all along.

———————————————

i once begged someone to stay
not knowing that if they left
i'd finally discover the peace
of being left behind

it's scary at first
absence leaves a void
but what if that emptiness
is just a space made
for something better

_____

i want to break this silence
but i can never find the words

———————————————

Your absence will prepare me for something better.

———————————————

Fear not the loss of what was never meant
to be yours.

———————————————

Being alone is preferable to being surrounded by the people who only intend to cause you harm.

Thank you for your absence. You left, and yet nothing was missing.

———————————

It's ironic how silence can be the most
deafening noise.

The loneliest parts of your life are an opportunity to delve deep within and rediscover the beauty of your own company.

————————————————

tired of nightmares
so tonight
she'll sleep less

restless and haunted
many questions, no answers

what does it all mean
the terror in her dreams

———————————————

I think loneliness can be transformative. Oftentimes
something great can be created within the spaces of
solitude, whether it be a material thing that can be
felt or a strength that resides deep in the mind, heart,
and or soul. The origin of something powerful and
beautiful can be cultivated in the absence of others.

I speak from experience because that's where I often
found myself, in the corners, almost hiding, shaded
by shadows cast by familiar feelings of betrayal. And
in my pursuit of someone to trust, I found a mirror,
and in it I saw the reflection of the only person
deserving of all that I have to offer: me.

———————————

It is in the soul's solo dance of discovery that loneliness, the silent teacher, reveals the power that you embody to cultivate love for yourself even in the wake of rejection of someone you thought you'd spend your future with.

———————————

The peace of solitude is a place where one's inner thoughts can develop and flourish.

When heartache ends, peace comes. When toxic love is severed, the heart begins to walk a path that leads to peace of mind and the hope for something better.

_____

Sometimes a person's absence is a beautiful gift. It's wild to think that the person who is trying to hurt you has only helped you realize that life is so much better without them in it.

—————————————

As soon as I had entered the realm of solitude, it was
as if the world around me suddenly transformed into
a blank canvas filled with unexplored opportunities.
The same stillness that had before threatened
to suffocate me was now gently cradling me in
its embrace. This has made it possible for me to
reestablish a connection with my authentic self,
free from the stress of living up to the expectations
of others. It was as if I had stumbled onto a hidden
garden deep within my spirit where I could tend
to my dreams and desires with gentle care and
undivided concentration.

My spirit was suffocated, and my heart was shackled
when I was in the wrong relationship; so, when it
ended, I felt a great feeling of liberation. I was freed
from the chains that had been holding me back. I was
no longer tethered to a love that wasn't meant for me,
and as a result, I was free to investigate the depths
of my passions and the breadth of my possibilities
when I was by myself. The peace and quiet of being
by myself helped me recognize the value of self-love
and personal development, which in turn enabled me
to carve a new route toward a future that was in every
sense entirely mine.

In the wide emotional bridge of loneliness, we often find that we have grown attached to the silent but throbbing weight of isolation, which is a lovely torture space we have made for ourselves.

Even in this harsh place, we can find the hidden gems of self-discovery, self-love, and strength, as well as the unexpected joys that come from being alone. As we learn to handle the rough terrain of being alone for the first time, our hearts fill with the unshakeable courage to stand alone, and we grow with the strength to keep going through it all. We learn to treasure the times when our souls dance in the silence, a symphony of self-love and freedom ringing from the lonely chambers of our once-empty hearts, when we welcome the paradoxical embrace of loneliness. We find the delicate balance between pain and pleasure in the bittersweet hug of solitude, and we learn to fly on the wings of our own freedom.

Letting go is a painfully beautiful thing.

———————————————

I think it was harder to find myself with you always
standing in my way. When I set out to search for love,
I had no idea that it would someday mean looking
past you. All this time, I had thought you left me
behind, but in truth, everything I always deserved
was just waiting in the distance behind you, and
to get closer to my dreams, I had to say no to the
nightmarish war of loving you.

There is an inner voice that means to tell you the
secret to life and the way toward the love you deserve,
and every time you leave a person who hurts you,
that voice becomes louder. You have to walk away so
that you can understand.

---

you ping-pong between emotions
only there is no table
and the ping-pong paddles
are fists wearing brass knuckles

———————————————

TRUTH IN SORROW & LESSON LEARNED

Know the difference between someone giving you
space and someone abandoning you.

_____

Are you the one they want, or are you the only one available at the moment . . .

He doesn't miss you; he's just horny.

———————————————

Not always getting what we desire can be a blessing in disguise.

———————————————

Express gratitude for the challenging individuals in your life, and gain wisdom from them. They have illuminated what kind of person you do not wish to become.

The same person who can offer you a glimpse of
paradise can also expose you to the depths of despair.

_____

Set boundaries. Stop compromising your peace
of mind to hold on to people who make you feel
unworthy of their consideration and time.

———————————

Your ex has nothing authentic to share. Don't go back.

———————————————

You struggle to see them for who they truly are because you fell in love with their potential.

———————————————————

Wanting to feel safe is not asking for too much.

———————————————

As you grow and evolve, some individuals, relationships, environments, and possessions may no longer align with the person you are becoming. It is important to prioritize the growth and development of your authentic self, even if it means letting go of certain aspects of your life.

———————————

Healing is a journey that requires time, persistence, and all of your effort. Be patient with yourself.

_____

You can't build your dreams with a man who is
content with being a nightmare.

The right relationship will not require you to feel
confused about where you stand in your partner's life.

_____

Relationships thrive on trust. If you find yourself
constantly having to investigate your partner, it may
be time to reevaluate the relationship.

———————————————

The idea of spending the rest of your life with someone else may seem romantic and idyllic, but it's essential to remember that, before we can commit to another person, we must first learn to be content with ourselves. To spend the rest of your life with someone requires a deep and unwavering commitment, and this commitment must be built on a foundation of self-love and self-acceptance.

Learning to be alone is a critical aspect of building a healthy relationship with oneself. It's about learning to enjoy your own company, to be comfortable in your own skin, and to find happiness in the little moments of life. When you've learned to love yourself and find joy in your own company, you'll find that you have much more to give to others in your life.

When we are content and at peace with ourselves, we are better able to connect with others on a deeper level. We bring a sense of calm and tranquility to our relationships, and we are less likely to become dependent on our partners for our own happiness. So, before you commit to spending the rest of your life with someone else, take the time to build a strong and loving relationship with yourself first. The journey of self-discovery is a lifelong one, but it's a journey that's well worth taking.

———————————

Desperation can cloud our vision, leading us to make decisions that we may later regret. It's easy to become so consumed with the desire to be loved that we lose sight of what truly matters. We become blinded by the need for validation and acceptance, and we may not see the warning signs that indicate that the love we're seeking is not forthcoming.

In the search for love, we may find ourselves drawn to people who are not capable of loving us in the way we deserve. They may be incapable of understanding our needs or may be too consumed with their own issues to give us the attention we crave. We may not see the truth, even when it's staring us in the face.

It's only when we step back and take a closer look that we begin to see the reality of the situation. We see that the love we thought we wanted is not the love we need. We realize that the most important person to love us is ourselves, and we start to build a sense of self-worth that no one else can take away.

It's a difficult lesson to learn, but it's one that's essential if we want to live a life filled with love and joy. We must be willing to let go of the need for validation and acceptance and learn to love ourselves first. Only then can we attract the kind of love that will sustain us and enrich our lives.

When we've been hurt, it's natural to seek out comfort and healing from those who we thought we could trust. We may look to them to provide solace and relief, but often this is a fruitless endeavor. For, those who broke us cannot heal us, and seeking healing at their feet is an exercise in futility.

It's difficult to accept that the people who we once looked up to and trusted are no longer capable of giving us what we need. It's hard to let go of the hope that they will change and start treating us with the kindness and respect we deserve. But sometimes, we must learn to accept the truth and move on.

The path to healing is a personal journey, and it's one that we must undertake ourselves. We must learn to let go of those who broke us and, instead, focus on the people who can help us heal. It's important to surround ourselves with those who will uplift us, support us, and provide the love and care we need.

So do not look for healing from the hands of those who hurt you. Look instead to the people who can provide the love and care you deserve. Focus on yourself, and find the strength and courage to move forward. In time, you'll find that the healing you need is within you and that you can overcome even the deepest wounds.

Mistakes are a natural part of life, a stepping-stone toward growth and progress. However, sometimes we tend to cling to our mistakes, not wanting to let go of the time and effort we have invested in them. It's understandable to feel attached to something we have worked hard on, but holding on to a mistake can be detrimental to our growth and success.

Letting go of a mistake can be difficult, especially when it has consumed a lot of our time and energy. But it's important to remember that the time we spent making the mistake cannot be regained. Holding on to it only prolongs the negative impact it has on us and prevents us from moving forward and making better choices in the future.

It's not a sign of weakness to admit that we have made a mistake but rather a sign of strength and wisdom. By acknowledging our mistake, we can learn from it, grow, and apply the lessons we have learned to future situations. So don't cling to a mistake just because you have spent a lot of time making it. Instead, let go, and embrace the opportunity to start anew.

Mistakes are a valuable part of the learning process, but it's crucial to not get too attached to them. Letting go of our mistakes, no matter how much time and effort we have invested in them, can be a freeing and empowering experience that leads to growth, success, and happiness.

R.H. SIN

Breaking free from an emotionally abusive relationship can be a difficult and challenging experience, but it can also be incredibly rewarding. When you are in an abusive relationship, you may feel trapped, isolated, and powerless. However, once you gather the strength and courage to leave, you can start to reclaim your life and your sense of self-worth. You may begin to realize that you are capable of more than you thought, and you can start to pursue your own interests and goals. You may also be able to rebuild relationships with friends and family members who were pushed away during the abusive relationship. Ultimately, breaking free from an emotionally abusive relationship can lead to a sense of liberation, self-discovery, and the ability to cultivate healthier relationships in the future.

With maturity, you learn to appreciate the things you have in this life and the people in it. Don't be fooled by all the usernames, content, photos, and videos. You may think you have options, but most of that is not profound. Just ask anybody . . . there's not much out there but more of what you don't want. If you should ever meet someone who genuinely cares for your soul, someone who inquires about your last meal, someone who loves you through all your ups and downs and changes . . . Someone who sees the version of you that YOU don't share here on your feed, the part of you that most people have deemed unlovable, the part of you that most people force you to feel like you have to hide . . . If you find someone who loves every inch of you as if they've laid eyes on perfection, love them and never let them go, or at the very least, appreciate the fact that you have found heaven amid hell, peace in the middle of chaos.

I'm flawed in many ways, but I think I have a superpower; I have this ability to be the most consistent thing in a lifetime if I'm allowed the opportunity to do so, and I think there are many of you reading this right now who share that same ability. My advice to you is to not let heartbreak change that. Don't let anyone who isn't for you change or distract you from the path leading to the one. Don't lose who you are because of someone who thought it was okay to lose you.

——————————————

Most people will not be able to comprehend the value of your presence in their lives, but that's okay, because you are not for everyone.

———————————————

It's easy to be taken in by a beautiful mind, by the intelligence and quick wit that some people possess. But what good is a brilliant intellect if it's not tempered by a beautiful heart? The ability to love, to care for others, to show kindness and compassion— these are the qualities that make life worth living. To discover a beautiful heart in someone is a true gift, a treasure that is priceless and immeasurable.

On the other hand, to come to the realization that someone may have neither a beautiful mind nor a beautiful heart is a tragedy. It's heartbreaking to see someone who's incapable of caring for others, who's consumed by their own desires and interests. Such individuals may have all the wealth, knowledge, and power in the world, but it's all for nothing if they lack a heart that's capable of loving and giving.

In the end, what truly matters is the legacy that we leave behind, the impact we make on the lives of those around us. It's not enough to be smart or successful; we must also be kind and caring and have a heart that beats with love and empathy. So let us strive to discover the beauty within ourselves and others, and let that beauty guide us on our journey through life.

The rain may have stopped, but the pain remained,
A weight on my heart that left me feeling restrained.
With every step, it felt like an anchor, a chain,
Dragging me down, causing nothing but strain.

The rain had come and gone, leaving behind, A
reminder of the tears that had flowed from my mind.
But even as the clouds began to dissipate, The pain
remained, a constant and unyielding weight.

It's hard to explain the kind of hurt that lingers, Like
a wound that refuses to close, despite our fingers. The
kind of pain that seeps into our bones, And leaves us
feeling broken and all alone.

But perhaps there's something to be said for this
pain, A reminder of the trials and the strength we've
gained. For even in the darkest moments, we find
a way, To rise above the pain and the sorrow and
seize the day.

So even as the rain stops, the pain remains, A
reminder that life is not always sunshine and
rainbows sustained. But with each passing day, we
learn to bear the weight, And find the strength to
carry on, no matter the fate.

Loneliness, oh how it seeps into the soul, A bittersweet ache that takes its toll, A solitary path that few dare tread, A journey into the heart, where emotions are led. It's a quiet room with empty walls, A silence that echoes, a haunting call, A longing for connection that's not there, A yearning for love that seems so rare.

Yet in the midst of the emptiness, there's a beauty, A chance to reflect, to gaze upon life's duty, To delve into the depths of our being, To find solace in the feelings we're seeing. Loneliness, it's a journey of self-discovery, A chance to ponder on life's mystery, To find strength in the solitude that we face, And courage in the challenges we embrace.

It's a canvas for creativity, a chance to create, To delve into the depths of our inner state, To find meaning in the moments of our life, To write our own story, to embrace the strife.

Loneliness, it's not just an absence of others, But an invitation to discover, to uncover, The beauty and depth of our own existence, A chance to see life with new persistence. So let loneliness be a painful beauty, An introspective path, a journey of duty, For in the end, we're never truly alone, As long as we have the courage to make our own.

You poison your future by living in the past.

———————————————

The in-between times are the worst. I hope to let go,
but I want to hold on.

It is painful to end a relationship. But the pain that results from losing oneself in a relationship is perhaps worse.

_____

When you've been injured so badly, it's hard to find
the words to express how you feel.

Discovering who you are as a person is the
prerequisite to stumbling onto your other half.

Human emotions are like a complicated tapestry that can tie us to places that have left scars on our hearts. Even in the middle of pain and trouble, nostalgia weaves a subtle thread of desire. Even if we hate the ground that was there when we were hurt, we may still want to feel its comfortable embrace. It is in these times of conflict that we realize how bittersweet memories are. A place we don't like can be both a haunting ghost and a safe haven, where shadows of the past stay among soft whispers of what was once home.

Just as a bird can soar above the clouds of yesterday
by releasing its grip on the day's winds, so too can we
let go of the past and embrace the infinite possibilities
of the here and now.

—————————————

It's important not to dwell on what could have
happened in the past. We should instead focus
on going forward and living in the here and now,
learning from our mistakes and trying to do better in
the future.

———————————

All my life, I have felt a pull toward something greater, a longing for something just beyond my reach. It whispers to me in the quiet moments, whispers of a life filled with purpose and fulfillment. I cannot name it, but I know that my heart will never be fully at peace until I find it. I search for it every day, driven by the hope that, one day, I will finally discover what it is that my heart has been yearning for all these years.

In the pursuit of love, it can be easy to lose oneself
and become consumed by the needs and desires of
another. But when we give too much of ourselves,
sacrificing our own happiness and identity in the
process, that is when the true pain sets in. For it
is then that we realize we have forgotten our own
worth, the unique qualities that make us special and
deserving of love. It's a harsh lesson but one that
reminds us to never lose sight of who we are and to
always prioritize our own well-being, even in the
midst of loving someone deeply.

_____

As we journey through life, we often underestimate our own strength and potential. We limit ourselves with our self-doubt and insecurities, not realizing the vastness of our own character. But then there comes a moment when we are faced with challenges, and we rise to the occasion, surprising even ourselves with our resilience and compassion. In these moments, we discover that we are larger, better than we thought; we are capable of so much more than we ever imagined. And it is then that we come to understand that within us lies an abundance of goodness, waiting to be unleashed and shared with the world.

In life, we often face difficulties and hardships that can feel overwhelming and unbearable. But it's important to remember that these experiences shape us and help us to grow. They test our strength and resilience and push us to become the best version of ourselves. From the pain and the struggles, a new, stronger, and wiser person will emerge. And that person will be you, having emerged from the hardships with a clearer understanding of your own worth and a greater appreciation for life. So hold on to hope, for the person you will become will be the result of everything you are going through.

Sadness is the black smoke that rises from the flames
of my shattered dreams.

———————————

The loss of love echoes through my bones, a constant ache that no amount of tears can wash away.

Love can be a fiery inferno or a frozen wasteland, a
journey to the depths of hell or the heights of heaven.

———————————————

I'm not really sure where it went wrong, an entire future destroyed by choice. A choice presented as a mistake, but that was all a lie. You see, you took your time, setting fire to everything we were attempting to build, and still you believed that I should forget. You painted false pictures of regret, telling yourself that you're a prize, but it's funny because you don't act like it.

———————————

The problem is that when you are cold and empty,
you hurt others, and when you are sensitive and full
of feelings, you get hurt.

———————————

The moon appears at midnight, creating a ghostly white glow around the room. The fire explodes and crackles, creating shadows on the wall. Here I am, all by myself, feeling sad and insignificant. I thought I had it all—I even thought I had found love—but now all I have is dust and ashes. As I sit here, alone and despised, the flames dance before my eyes as if to mock my suffering.

Even if you're in a committed relationship, the pain of isolation might feel like an open sore that will never heal. I was sure I could make it, that I would be okay, but now I have nothing and am struggling to stay alive.

The moon seems to be watching over me, saying, "I know your pain, I've been alone too, night and day." As I sit here in the dark with nothing but my broken heart and the embers of a dying fire, I can't help but feel a pang of loss.

But I must press on; I must keep going, even though my heart is broken and my spirit is being tormented. The fire will start up again; the moon will shine brighter; and maybe, just maybe, my broken heart will mend enough to allow love once more.

When I was trying to show you something different,
you didn't want it. My effort was wasted, and my
devotion was never enough. I guess it takes time to
see value in something you once had, especially when
the thing you chose turned out to be nothing. I was
always this, the thing you see, the thing you miss. I
was always me, overlooked by you.

too important to lose
and yet you lost me
too good for this shit
so when i leave
i won't feel bad

———————————

you lied to me
to protect my feelings
but in the end
my heart aches
with the realization
that you believed
that i didn't deserve
the truth

———————————————

i just think
waiting for
the wrong person
to love you
is like waiting
for it to rain
in hell

when you discover the lie
you question everything
you once believed to be true

———————————————

You suffocated my self-worth, then judged me for lacking confidence.

---

you were trying to hurt me
when you left
but in time, i realized
that you were only
returning me to a place
where i could find someone better
someone with more to offer
than what you were willing to give

_____

Your essence is powerful, and not everyone is ready for it. Some people may find your authenticity overwhelming or be unable to handle the depth of emotion and passion that you bring to the table. They may feel threatened or intimidated by your confidence and inner strength.

But that doesn't mean that you should dull your shine or hide your true self. Your light is important, and it has the power to inspire and uplift others who are on a similar path.

Just be mindful of who you share it with. Not everyone deserves your time, energy, and essence. Focus on surrounding yourself with people who appreciate and support you and who are willing to do the inner work necessary to connect with you on a deeper level.

And, most importantly, don't let anyone make you feel like you need to diminish yourself in order to be accepted or loved. You are worthy and deserving of love just as you are, and anyone who can't see that is not worth your time or energy.

To be intimate requires more than just physical contact or experiences that are common to both parties. It is about seeing and being understood on a level that is deeper than words can express.

When you are truly intimate with someone, you are able to communicate with them even when words are not necessary. It's about discovering a sense of connection and comprehension in the still moments, even while the rest of the world is a chaotic mess around you.

It hurts because you genuinely give a damn.

———————————

There are times when the soul makes an investment
in the wrong person.

———————————————

Seeking refuge in the embrace of the person who is often the source of your suffering and sadness is never going to bring you a sense of safety.

———————————

Stop rewarding foolish behavior. Your presence is a gift. You are meant to leave behind anyone who fails to comprehend or see the value you add to their lives.

_____

I have faith that you are capable of meeting the requirements of letting go and moving on for good.

You have the ability to free yourself, regardless of the obstacles that stand in your way. The alleviation of your suffering is one of my highest priorities, and I really hope that you find some solace in my words.

———————————————

To be able to let go of something or someone, you must realize and accept the fact that they will always be a part of your past but will never be a part of your future.

I think in the end you finally see what you missed in the beginning. People wear masks, some of them out of fear or from being vulnerable while others are just pretending to be the type of person worthy of your attention. Oftentimes, it is the ending that tells you everything you wish to know about the person you thought you'd spend the rest of your life with. You either see someone who didn't have the tools to make it work or you're faced with the fact that the person you invested your energy into never actually intended to stay. Either ending provides the opportunity to find something else to pour your love into, and more times than not, the person most deserving of all that you have to offer is yourself.

It's a tough realization, that moment of understanding that you wasted valuable time on someone who didn't intend to value you, but in the end, you learn a valuable lesson in two parts: one, you are stronger than you previously realized, and two, you now know what and who to avoid moving forward.

The end of any relationship reminds us that love is not enough if it extends only from one side; half love will never lead to a relationship that feels full of light and love. When the energy you invest into a relationship isn't reciprocated, that energy can't survive. And not all endings are the same. Some of them hurt in the deepest of ways, while some provide a sense of relief and power.

The end can be a disaster, a fiery inferno, a place of visual destruction. The end can also be a safe haven or a beautiful garden, where new and profound things can grow.

The end can be filled with doubt and be met with fear, but on the other hand, the end can give way to new ideas of love; it can be a place where something better can begin to bloom.

Whatever your ending has become, let me remind you that there is still an opportunity to begin again, and in time, no matter how difficult this may feel, you will be fine.

When you're done getting angry, you're closer to letting go. You see no need to fight with this person because you realize that they are no longer worth fighting for. You save your energy once you know that sharing that energy with them is a waste of time, and so when you're done getting upset, you daydream about letting go. I speak from experience, as I can still remember the relationships of my past and how I left with a sort of ease that would suggest that I didn't care in the first place . . . but that's the thing. Sometimes you care so much that being mistreated and disrespected and suffering a feeling of lack of appreciation drives you up a wall and sometimes closer to an exit.

Some of us are so used to being on the opposite end of mistreatment, and so we deal with it over an extended amount of time because we've grown strong enough to tolerate it. And often we stay with a person not out of love but simply because we can bear the harm of loving the wrong person. I've been guilty of trying harder when I should have quit. I've had my share of disappointment from investing hope in a hopeless situation. I've even stayed in a relationship because I believed that I was suitable for that person, even knowing they were wrong for me, but there comes a moment in the matrix when you wake up and realize that peace can be cultivated only in the absence of the person you were trying to make peace with.

When it's done, you'll know. You'll feel relieved at the idea of walking away. You'll begin to reason with yourself with a newfound clarity; you'll stitch a silver lining as you figure out that, all this time, you were just too good of a person for someone who only intended to make you feel bad. And the best thing about it is that you'll owe them no explanation as you gather your things to move forward with your life. This year has been a rough year for some, and it isn't over yet; if there were lessons to learn this year, it's that nothing is promised and life is fragile. Do not waste another moment on people who drain you of your peace of mind and distract you from the love you deserve.

It's so easy to daydream about a life outside your own, but it's important to be present and to appreciate everything your life currently is. I outgrew the part of me that looks over at the way others live. I've outgrown the part of me that dreams of something more while neglecting what I already have. Be here, be present, be now. Be here because this is a beautiful start, despite whatever obstacles you've faced. Never want what someone else has, because you have no idea what they had to do to get those things; oftentimes, if you did, you'd realize that FOR YOU, IT ISN'T WORTH IT.

There is nothing more beautiful than the present, because it is here that you have life and the opportunity to pursue more of your purpose. It is here, in this moment, where most of what you love and enjoy exists. Life is so fragile. Yours and my own. Tomorrow is not promised. Appreciate where you are, and make it beautiful.

Someday, when you look back on this moment
of your life, you will see it as a bittersweet time
of grieving. You may remember the tears that
fell like rain and the pain that remained in your
heart, but you will also remember the way your life
was changing.

In those moments of sadness, you may have felt like
everything was falling apart, but little did you know,
you were being molded into someone new. The
struggles and heartaches you endured were preparing
you for the future, a future filled with opportunities
and blessings beyond your wildest dreams.

You may not have seen it then, but your grief was
a catalyst for growth. You learned to persevere
through the toughest of times, to hold on to hope
when all seemed lost, and to cherish the love that
surrounded you.

So when you look back on this moment, you will
see that although it was painful, it was also a time
of great transformation. You will be grateful for the
lessons learned and for the person you have become
because of them. Your heart may have been broken,
but it was also mended, stronger and more resilient
than ever before.

———————————

Life is full of ups and downs, turns and surprises you didn't expect. We often think about what could have been or what we could have done differently and get stuck there. But sometimes we have to let go of the past in order to move forward.

We can choose not to think about what's gone and instead focus on what's still here. We can be thankful for the good memories, the lessons we've learned, and the people who have been there for us through it all. We can keep the things in our lives that make us happy and give us hope for the future.

It can be both exciting and scary to think about what will happen next. It's normal to be afraid of what we don't know, but we can choose to see it as a chance to learn and try new things. Every new thing we do gives us the chance to learn, discover, and make a better future for ourselves and those around us.

Let go of what's holding you back, be grateful for what you still have, and look forward to what's next. Life is a journey, and it's up to us to enjoy every step of the way.

Despite my certainty that you didn't call, I double-checked, nevertheless.

———————————

Scars are reminders of the many times our cries
for help went unheard by those we thought we
needed the most.

———————————

In my immaturity, I was unable to love her properly.

_____

However, there came a point when I no longer cared about not seeing you.

―――――――――――――

At other times, the peace and quiet of being alone is preferable to the agony of trying to explain yourself over and over to people who will never get it.

———————————————

With time, the world's constant tugging at my heartstrings left me torn to the point at which I came undone.

Our version of forever was so fucking brief. Our happily ever after was the saddest end of all.

When they ask you where I am, I hope you tell them
that you fucking lost me.

I used to build my future on you.

Both the way I loved you and the way you broke me
were tragically beautiful.

———————————

Because of our hardwired need for familiarity, if the only thing we've ever known is suffering, that's what we'll pick.

———————————

Once you've learned something, it's like a seed that refuses to be uprooted from your mind and changes the way you perceive the world forever.

———————————————

It's as if you're always losing people you never had.

_____

I care about you, but you refuse to try for me;
therefore, I can't keep trying to make things
better for us.

―――――――――――――

Mourning the past is a surefire way to ruin your future.

Perhaps you need to have experienced a dreadful night in order to fully value the meaning of a new morning.

———————————————

It is important to correct the conditions in which a flower grows rather than the flower itself if it does not bloom. You have always been more than enough, and maybe it's time to remove the people in your life who have made it harder for you to fully bloom.

It's okay to be alone; it's okay to prefer it.

Damage still exists even after healing occurs. It signifies you are free from the hold of whatever or whoever wanted to tear you down.

———————————————

My eyes have grown tired of looking toward you as
you stare into a screen in search of everything I'd
willingly provide. And one day, you'll look up to see
that I've left you.

I genuinely hope that you experience moments of profound appreciation for life. I hope that a piece of your heart remains there always.

———————————————

And it's the most stunning sight I've ever seen, that
there is something like you in my universe.

The painful realization that the love you once thought was real was all in your head is like sand slipping through your fingers when you're trying to hold on to it. It leaves your heart dry and longing for something more real.

———————————————

a lie is the quickest way
to kill a heart

———————————

books can be umbrellas
you open one
and it nearly guards you
from a rainstorm of heartache

It's best not to explain everything all the time.

It is very unsettling to see how convincingly people can pretend.

———————————

People are altered through suffering.

———————————

Never beg someone for what you are entitled
to receive.

Learn to say no without shame or regret.

———————————

Every heartbreak is a gift; every moment of pain and or sadness laced with regret is a lesson. You learn the most powerful things when a person attempts to hurt you, and though you fear the pain, it is still the very thing that reminds you that you are strong enough to thrive under the harshest of conditions.

———————————————

There is no such thing as a minor lie.

The truth will always live inside a person's actions, no matter what they say or how often they say it. See a person for what they do, not what they speak.

_____

The end is never really the end. Something ends to give life to the possibility of a better beginning.

———————————————

There are people who will lie about their sadness.
They'll project their misery onto you, and whenever
you attempt to be there for them, they'll pretend to
be fine. Not because they're afraid of being vulnerable
but because they want you to keep them company in
their anguish. These types of people.

Telling someone you're okay and then projecting your
sadness, depression, or hurt onto them is toxic.

It's emotional abuse.

What's wild is that the same person will hurt
people and then claim that they hurt others
because they were hurting and no one was there for
them—bullshit.

_____

This unsettling and mostly indescribable feeling overwhelms you almost instantly when you're in the presence of someone undeserving of your energy, and it always takes too long to realize it. I mean, you feel it, but you don't necessarily know what it is until it's too late. This is what I've come to learn in my experience of caring for someone who didn't genuinely care for me. And when that feeling catches up to your comprehension, it hits you like a ton of emotionally threatening bricks. Somehow you saw it coming, but you were also blind to the impending doom.

HER CHAPTER, HER SONG

This section is dedicated to her alone, to the person whose eyes are moving gently from left to right across the page in pursuit of a deeper knowledge of who she is and what she is capable of becoming. These lines are an ode to the most resilient person I know: you.

———————————————

The lonely girl found a rich tapestry of self-discovery in the quiet embrace of solitude. The fullness of her own company grew like a beautiful, complicated flower, with each petal revealing a new aspect of her soul's beauty.

———————————

She told stories with her eyes, tales of knowledge gained through the losses of those she believed would always love her. The tears she cried, like chapters of what it took to survive the war of loving and fighting for the wrong person. This story, her story, though not easily read, deserves to be recognized and her courage rewarded for figuring out how to survive even on days where she believed she couldn't go on any longer.

The seeds of change she nurtures will grow into a legacy of limitless possibilities, and she blooms in the garden of life with resilience and courage, her vivid colors painting the world with the essence of empowerment.

Embrace the brilliance of your inner self; it brings strength and wisdom to the world and encourages others to do the same.

―――――――――――

She devoted her entire being to loving him, but
somewhere along the road, she lost sight of the fact
that she too was somebody and that she too deserved
to be loved.

———————————————

I know you; you're the girl with a painful story to tell.
A story that has gone on to transform you into more
of what you never thought you'd become. But here
you are, after all the tragedy, with the strength of a
triumphant warrior.

———————————————

Nurture your inner beauty, and let it shine, regardless
of those who don't appreciate it.

————————————————

She held on to her love for him but also held on to the painful truth that it may never be returned. It was a bittersweet existence, a constant dance between hope and despair. Yet, despite the hurt, she found beauty in the strength it took to keep going, to keep loving, even when it wasn't reciprocated. For, in the end, love is never truly lost; it only transforms into something different and possibly something else for someone else, someone willing to match and return what is felt and given. Right now, that someone is you.

She saw his potential. He saw an opportunity to
waste yet another woman's time. She loved him with
everything she had, only to realize that, in the end, he
was always nothing pretending to be something he
wasn't brave enough to be.

you hold her hand
you touch the future
you stare into her eyes
and see the depth of time

her aura was the future
her value, greater than numbers
words struggled to describe her
the present could not contain her

———————————

A woman is like a beautiful garden, with the power to grow and bloom in all seasons. Her beauty is both delicate and strong, with the ability to nourish and sustain life. Like a garden, she is a source of wonder and inspiration, full of color, fragrance, and vitality. And, like a garden, a woman's strength and resilience is often tested by the storms of life, but she emerges victorious and even more stunning, a testament to the power of nature and the human spirit. Truly, a woman is a garden of grace and beauty, a treasure to be cherished and nurtured.

The brokenness within her gave birth to her beauty.

———————————————

she radiated beauty wherever she went
she was a walking masterpiece
she was a work of art in motion
she was a living, breathing artistic revolution

―――――――――――――

The flower that flourishes in the face of adversity is a rare and stunning sight. Its beauty is born from overcoming challenges and hardships, making it all the more precious. This flower serves as a reminder that, even in the most difficult of circumstances, there is the potential for growth and grace. It symbolizes hope and resilience, inspiring us to continue on, even when the path ahead is uncertain.

she's a heavenly hellfire
a beautiful flame
a myth that came true

nothing about her is ordinary
she will not settle for mediocrity

You are a sunflower; you give energy, food, and shade to everyone in your garden.

———————————————

A woman who discovers self-love has found infinite knowledge of who she can truly be.

———————————————

a woman waking up
is a poem coming to life

———————————————

she
a rainstorm
i didn't mind getting wet

----

on nights
when i lie
restless
i long for
the meditation
between her thighs

a woman's strength is not to be underestimated
for in her lies a power that is eternal
the ability to give, love, and nurture endlessly
without any dismissals

she is a force to be reckoned with
and her grace will always move mountains
and destroy obstacles

never underestimate a woman
for she holds the power of infinite giving
she is a protector and provider
she is a promise of salvation

—————————

Despite the heartbreak, she rebuilt her kingdom upon the ruins of her heart. Fortifying the walls around her soul with the lessons she learned after being betrayed.

—————————————

she was silent
not because she was numb
but because she wanted
to keep the fire inside

———————————

they overlook you
because you've felt broken
they can't comprehend
the fact that when
they stand in your presence
they are witnessing art
in its purest form

———————————————

i know love
can be dangerous
but YOU AND I
will make it safe

i know love
can be wild
may i be free
with you

---

she stood alone but strong
and created the world
she had always imagined

she built a powerful kingdom
with her own two hands
and nothing could stop her

through strength and perseverance
she built a world that was uniquely her own

---

she had a way of seeing beyond the surface
to a world where strength and hope
was more than just a purpose

despite the sorrows
and the pain she had known
her spirit was an undying flame
continuing to grow

with each new dawn, she found something to believe in
a light that shone from within and kept her heart beaming

even when the world seemed lost in darkness and strife
she saw the potential, the beauty that was hidden in life

and that is what i loved the most about her
the way she held on to hope
as it dwelled within her soul

a magic that lit up the night
like a phoenix taking flight

in her undying hope, i found a source of strength
a reminder that life can be beautiful, despite its length
and even in the darkest of moments, there's a chance to rise

to find the good and believe in the magic of life's surprise

beneath her navel
a garden of roses
between her thighs

she breeds salvation
a truth that severs lies

———————————

She distanced herself to preserve her own well-being.

———————————

She is thunder, a danger to some but a light for those willing to look past their fear.

———————————

soft petals open
seeing her inner strength
goddess blooms in ecstasy

———————————————

I truly believe that a woman's love can turn a man's
page into chapters' worth of knowledge, power,
and beauty.

Even though she was in a dark place, she found her
own light and grew into a powerful flower.

————————————————

she glows like the moon
in the dark of night
her curves and edges
bathed in soft blue light

mysterious and enigmatic
her beauty serene
a celestial goddess
a beautifully rare dream

She is a treasure trove of enlightening secrets, waiting to be unlocked by a deserving someone.

_____

goddess in motion
her aura ignites my soul
magic in her touch

From the ashes of a broken heart rises a phoenix of self-love that soars high. With each heartbreak, a new layer of resilience blooms everlastingly.

She turned pain into a lesson. She realized your absence was a blessing.

———————————————

Stop losing sleep over a man who is likely sleeping with someone else while you're restless and alone.

―――――――――――――

She always loved the rain, especially at her lowest,
because she could stand in the middle of a storm
without an umbrella, and as the rain ran over and
down her face, no one knew that she'd been crying
the entire time.

When Mother Nature settled, she'd dry herself off
and then smile on her way back home. Full of doubt,
tired, and broken, but no one ever saw the sadness.

she blossomed in her own way
unrestricted by society's rules
like a wildflower in a meadow
a sight to witness and cherish

her spirit is as free as the wind
and her bold, vibrant hues
a wonder to behold
and a testament to nature's resiliency

she is you . . .

_____

A woman's strength radiates warmth,
summer's embrace.

She had the strength to move past the betrayal she
had suffered at the hands of someone she trusted.
She eventually bandaged her wounds and learned
to put her energy toward her own development and
well-being. Instead of letting the betrayal define her,
she embraced it to propel her forward. And like the
mythical phoenix, she arose from the ashes more
powerful, resilient, and resolved to succeed than ever
before. Taking responsibility for her recovery gave
her a renewed feeling of purpose and confidence in
her own strength.

What she learned from her suffering was a beautiful
and uplifting symphony of lessons and strength.

Despite her numerous setbacks in love, she remained
a lady of unyielding conviction. Despite the fact that
she was met with evidence that the love she sought
did not exist, she did not give up on her hopes.
She held out hope for the kind of love that would
fire her soul. And though the road was long and
winding, she knew the destination would be well
worth the effort in the end, for nothing but genuine
affection would do.

The strength of a woman is like the unyielding light of a goddess, and her will is like that of a mighty warrior.

———————————————

The self-confident woman dances like a rare
and captivating storm, setting fire to everything
in her path.

———————————————

The power of a woman ebbs and flows like the vast ocean, the depth of her wisdom like the abyss, the grace of her soul like the beauty and movement of the waves.

———————————

The entrancing flame of self-discovery that is an awakened woman burns away everything that no longer serves her and shines a fierce, empowering light down her chosen path.

———————————

A woman's spirit sings a beautiful melody that
harmonizes with the changing song of life. Every note
she creates makes you think of change and growth.

———————————————

In her vast presence, a woman embodies the whole
universe, bringing together celestial forces with grace,
power, and wisdom that never ends.

————————————————

Even after being broken, the strong woman
puts herself back together into a beautiful
mosaic that shows her newfound strength and
unwavering courage.

———————————————

A woman is like a sun-shower in that she combines the elements of warmth and rain to produce a beautiful dance of light and rejuvenation.

_____

The songs sung by a woman's broken heart are magnificent tragedies that speak to the depths of human experience and emotional transformation.

―――――――――――――

As a bird learning to fly, she soars toward her potential, spreading her wings to take hold of the success that she justly deserves.

She breaks free from the vicious cycle of grief with dignity and bravery, welcoming the regenerative dawn of self-love and independence.

———————————————

Tired of waiting for the proper love to come along,
she focused her energies inward, tapping into an
endless well of strength and devotion.

Eventually, the woman concerned with her obstacles realizes she has always been strong enough to move mountains with a glance.

———————————

There was a fire in her eyes that made the stars insignificant.

———————————

She is the awakening of truth and brilliance. There is a trail of genius left behind by her feet as she travels toward a life and love that is tailor-made for a woman of her caliber.

———————————————

she's tired of being hidden
she's tired of being a secret
gaslit and lied to
betrayed, then comforted
with empty promises of change

she's tired of feeling like she's settled
she's tired of fighting a war
she'll never win

she's tired of being tired of you

in the harshness of winter
she found a way to bloom
she gave new meaning to survival

———————————

love runs deepest
in those shattered hearts
of good women

———————————————

Most guys don't deserve your brilliance, but you shine forth anyhow.

———————————

The power of a woman lies not only in her resilience
but also in her will to succeed in the face of adversity.

———————————————

In order to make room for the right person in her life, the most beautiful thing a woman can do is to let go of the wrong one.

The burden of her troubles and the intensity of
her pain were things she kept to herself. She held
it all together, her heart marked by the wars she
had fought and the difficulties she had overcome.
She felt the anguish deep inside, yet she kept going
nevertheless.

She radiated power and strength, someone to be
taken seriously. She was the steadfast embodiment of
truth. She was the fighter, survivor, and warrior she
had always been. And she knew that, as long as she
kept her head up and her shoulders back, she could
handle anything that came her way.

She maintained her sense of self despite the many
obstacles she had to overcome. She was a tough
competitor who refused to give up. Her scars served
as a constant reminder that she was strong, not a
sign of her weakness. The woman looked in the
mirror and was greeted by a reflection of strength
and resolve.

In the face of naysayers, she demonstrated the
power of persistence and determination. She was an
inspiration who proved that the human will could
overcome enormous odds. And as she went on, she
knew she was sufficient in every manner, that she was
everything she'd ever wanted to be.

She had experienced tragedy and great suffering, but she would not be broken by it. Instead, she drew strength from adversity and developed resilience as a result of her experiences.

She kept going, even when hardships presented themselves. She instead tackled these difficulties head-on, aiming to grow as a person in the process. She overcame each challenge by gathering insight and experience that would serve her well in the future.

She emerged from her ordeal more resilient and stronger. She emerged from the experience with greater empathy, compassion, and awareness of the difficulties others faced. Because of this, she developed a strong capacity for compassion and an urge to aid those going through similar situations.

She was unwavering in her resolve to not let her suffering define who she was. Instead, she turned sorrow into motivation, utilizing it to forge herself into a more robust individual.

She persevered through hardship and emerged stronger for it. She emerged from her ordeal more resilient and resolute than ever before, with a renewed sense of purpose and a profound understanding of the value of perseverance. She felt confident in her ability to tackle future difficulties with the same composure and fortitude that had gotten her through the tough times in the past.

She was a rose, the way she communicated beauty and strength with every moment that led her to bloom.

_____

A day will come when she no longer waits for you. She won't be waiting by the phone, wondering if you'll call or if she'll ever get an explanation for your absence. As an alternative, she will seize every opportunity and embrace every joy that life has to give.

She will remember you fondly and with a smile on her face as she continues on her journey. She'll never forget the times you made her laugh and smile, but she'll never forget the times you didn't show up or treated her with the dignity she deserved, either.

At that point, she'll know that she narrowly escaped disaster. She'll eventually realize that the relationship you shared wasn't good for either of you and that she deserves better than you could give her.

But she won't feel resentment or bitterness, even after coming to that conclusion. She will be thankful for the opportunities for self-improvement and for the confidence she received in overcoming adversity. And she'll be hopeful and optimistic about what the future holds.

She won't be waiting for you at the end, since she'll have already moved on. Even though it'll be tough, she'll know that she made the correct choice and is on the path to the joy and fulfillment she deserves.

Her heart is an infinite library of love and suffering, and it has within it the wisdom of a thousand lifetimes, with each tearstained page serving as a witness to her unshakable strength and resiliency. She emerges from each conflict with a spirit that has been honed to the extent that only the purest steel can achieve, her light shining brighter than it ever has, inspiring countless souls to find their own courage and to create their own stories of triumph and redemption.

My dearest stranger,

I don't know who you are, nor where you reside, but I feel the weight of your weary heart behind your eyes as you read these words. It is a burden I too struggle with, a burden that feels as heavy as a millstone. But do not despair, dear one. Love is a fickle mistress, sometimes selfish and cruel. She takes as much as she gives and often leaves us shattered and alone. But in that darkness, there is still light. There is hope.

I know it is hard to believe when the pain is fresh and the wounds are raw. But trust me when I say that the wrong person can never truly satisfy the ache within. That person is but a bandage on a broken bone, a temporary fix for a permanent problem.

You deserve more than that, my love. You deserve someone who sees you as you are, flaws and all, and loves you for it. Someone who knows the shape of your heart and fits perfectly into it, completing you in ways you never thought possible.

And I know that person is out there, waiting for you to find them. It may take time, and it may take plenty of tears, years of pain, but they are there, I promise you. So do not give up on love, my dear stranger. Do not let the darkness consume you. Keep searching, keep hoping, keep believing. For, in the end, love is always worth the risk. Genuine love, true love, will always be worth the journey.

Yours always, a stranger you trust

My dear,

I know that the journey toward healing is not an easy one. It is a path filled with twists and turns, with moments of light and moments of darkness. And yet you continue to walk it, one step at a time.

I want you to know that I see you, and I am proud of you. I am proud of the way you have faced your pain head-on, of the way you have refused to give up, even when it seemed like the weight of the world was on your shoulders. I know there are days when the ache within feels too much to bear, when the wounds of the past seem too deep to heal. But please, my dear, do not give up hope. You are stronger than you realize, more resilient than you can imagine.

And though the road may be long and the destination may seem far off, I believe that you will reach it. You will find peace, and you will find healing. You will emerge from this stronger, more whole, more beautiful than ever before. So do not lose heart, my love. Keep moving forward, one step at a time. And know that you are not alone. I am here, cheering you on, supporting you and loving you every step of the way.

With all my heart, always

_____

Dear woman,

I want you to know that you are deserving of love and respect just the way you are. You are beautiful, strong, and capable of achieving anything you set your mind to. Sometimes, it's easy to fall into the trap of self-doubt and self-criticism, but it's important to remember that your worth is not determined by your flaws or imperfections.

Self-love is a journey, and it takes time and effort to build a healthy relationship with yourself. It's okay to make mistakes and have bad days, but it's important to practice self-compassion and treat yourself with kindness and understanding. Surround yourself with people who lift you up and support you, and don't be afraid to seek help if you need it.

When it comes to romantic love, remember that you are not defined by your relationship status. You are complete and whole on your own, and any relationship you enter into should enhance your life, not define it. Don't settle for anything less than you deserve, and don't compromise your values or boundaries for anyone else.

Ultimately, you are the only person who can determine your worth and your happiness. So embrace your uniqueness, celebrate your strengths, and love yourself fiercely. You are capable of amazing things, and you deserve all the love and happiness in the world. Give it all to yourself.

If there's one thing I want you to know, it's this: Self-love is one of the most beautiful gifts you can give yourself. It's easy to think that our happiness and fulfillment lie in external sources—in our achievements, in the approval of others, in the material possessions we accumulate. But, the truth is, everything we've ever needed has been within us all along.

When we take the time to truly love ourselves, to embrace all of our quirks and flaws, we open up a world of possibility. We begin to see ourselves in a different light—as deserving of love and respect, just as we are. And with that shift in perspective comes a newfound confidence, a sense of purpose, and a deep sense of inner peace.

The journey of self-discovery can be challenging at times, but the rewards are immeasurable. As you learn to love and accept yourself, you'll begin to attract more positivity and abundance into your life. You'll form deeper, more meaningful relationships, and you'll feel empowered to pursue your passions and dreams without fear.

So I encourage you to take some time for yourself today/tonight/this week—to reflect on all the wonderful things that make you who you are and to embrace them fully. Remember that everything you need to live a happy, fulfilled life is already within you.

Take care of yourself. You are more powerful than you know.

My dear stranger,

I know not who you are, nor the depths of the sadness that you carry with you. But I can feel it, heavy and burdensome, in every word that you write. The weight of loneliness can be crushing, and I understand the weariness that comes from searching for love in a world that often feels so cruel and unyielding.

But, please, do not give up hope. Do not let the darkness consume you. There is love out there, waiting for you to find it. It may not be easy to find, and it may not be what you expected, but it is there, I promise you.

Sometimes, love comes in unexpected ways—in a kind word from a stranger, in the beauty of a sunset, in the sound of a bird singing outside your window. And, sometimes, it comes in the arms of another person who sees you as you are and loves you all the more for it.

I know it is hard to believe when the pain is so raw and the loneliness feels so all-encompassing. But trust me when I say that there is light at the end of the tunnel. There is a future when you are loved, when you are cherished, when you are not alone.

So do not give up, my dear stranger. Keep searching, keep hoping, keep believing. For, in the end, love is always worth the risk.

Sending you positive energy

Dear person struggling with self-love and healing,

I know that the journey of healing after losing someone you thought you'd spend a future with can be a difficult and painful one. It takes time, effort, and a lot of hard work. But know that you are not alone on this journey. I am here with you, every step of the way. It can be easy to feel lost in the pain of grief, but please remember that healing is not a linear process. There will be days when it feels like you've taken three steps forward and five steps back. That is okay. Healing is not a race. It is a journey, and every step you take is a step in the right direction.

Take the time you need to grieve. Allow yourself to feel the pain, the sadness, and the anger. But do not let them consume you. Remember that you are strong, resilient, and capable of healing. One of the most important things you can do on this journey is to be kind to yourself. Be patient, be gentle, and be forgiving. Healing takes time, and it is okay to take a step back when you need to.

Remember that healing is not about forgetting the person you lost but about learning to live without them. It is about finding a way to carry their memory with you while still moving forward with your life.

Always here for you

Dear woman,

You are not alone in feeling tired and weary from loving the wrong person. It takes courage and strength to love someone with all your heart, and when it doesn't work out, it can be a hard and painful experience.

But despite the hurt and disappointment, know that you are still capable of love, happiness, and a fulfilling life. You deserve someone who loves and respects you for who you are and who will cherish and support you every step of the way.

Take some time to heal, to be kind to yourself, and to rediscover your own worth and strengths. Remember that you are a beautiful, intelligent, and capable woman and that you deserve nothing but the best.

As you move forward, trust yourself and your instincts. Love yourself first, and be patient. The right person will come into your life when you least expect it, and they will bring joy, comfort, and a love that will last a lifetime.

Keep your head up and your heart open, and never give up on love. It is one of the greatest gifts life has to offer, and it is waiting for you.

With love and support, r.h. Sin

Dear woman,

Love hasn't forgotten about you. Through the
years, you have unknowingly wasted your time in
relationships that were not worthy of your energy.
You have shared yourself with individuals who were
never worthy of your presence and touch. Even so, love
hasn't forgotten about you. This year, remain faithful
to what brings you peace, and stay true to what helps
you grow and heal, even if that means being alone
for a while. There is nothing wrong with being alone,
especially when you've discovered that you are meant
for so much more and that you are no longer willing to
settle for a relationship that doesn't match up with all
that you are and all that you have to offer.

Let this be a sign of what will come when you decide
to be at peace with leaving behind the people who no
longer fit into your life or your idea of love. Let these
be the things you run back to whenever you struggle
with the idea of moving on. I want you to arrive
here whenever you feel lost; I want you to take your
seat here at the table, a place where you will not be
judged, a place where you find what you need. I want
you to be reminded that you are entirely enough,
even on your darkest day.

It is beautiful, your existence, the way you move
through the hurt, sometimes pausing to breathe in,
to take a moment, times when you feel stuck. It's
beautiful; you are reminded of how strong you are
whenever it feels like you can't go on, but you do, and
you're here right now, reading these words.

You are an inspiration, and I wrote this for you.

To the woman who decides to read this . . .

I hope you recover; I hope you find out that, despite the pain you've felt, this moment of heartache was an opportunity to find your voice.

To the woman reading this right now who feels stuck in a toxic relationship: I want you to remember that, in this life, you have always been able to move forward, refusing to stop even when you felt as if you couldn't go on.

To the woman who just received a text from an ex: Don't reply.

Did you know that when an ex sees you happy without them, they decide to send an "I miss you" text? They choose to manipulate you by popping back up during nights like this, nights when you may feel lonely, vulnerable, and even nostalgic. Don't allow yourself to reopen a book to a story that will just end the same way it did before.

To the woman who has given up hope in finding real love: Do not let people from your past dictate your future. Do not be held back from getting what you've given all because of the pain of sharing your love with someone who could never appreciate you fully.

I think it's easy to lose hope when you've grown tired of investing your energy into people who refuse to match it. Your idea of love is real, and it exists, but you will never find it until you find the strength to refuse to allow your life to be controlled by lovers who never loved you.

To the woman reading this who wonders if I'm talking to her: I am. I want to take this moment to thank you for being strong, for being an inspiration, and for not giving up on yourself. You're here now because there's a piece of you that still believes that love is real and that you are meant for so much more than what you've had.

We have a connection here; we're sharing the same wavelength. This here is a moment in time when we can all feel as if we're not alone. I am but one man, a stranger just looking for an opportunity to reach you and maybe inspire you to keep going, and hopefully I just did.

We bond here. We cry, we realize, we process, and we keep going. We connect, we feel, and we open up. This community, the people reading this right now, are all connected, and you have all inspired me over the years. All my life, strong women have surrounded me, and I would not be the man I am if it weren't for the women I grew up around, and this is my way of giving back, as you may have felt neglected or overlooked in your life or even invisible. This is my offering to you, though it isn't much. I give you my insight, some things I know, the things I've learned, and everything I've witnessed. So let's savor these moments, even though they're difficult. These lessons are challenging, but you will always find a way to come out the other side stronger than before, and I'm just glad I had the opportunity to share these things with you. And, hopefully, when I go away, you will remember everything I've said. I just want you to be happy. Reread this whenever you feel like giving up on yourself.

As the year moves forward, I want to remind you of your worth and strength. You have been through so much, and yet you still have the courage to open your heart and fall in love again. I know that it can be hard to trust and love again after falling for the wrong person, but don't let that pain dim the light of hope within you.

You are a rose, delicate and beautiful, with petals that unfurl in the warmth of love. And, just like a rose, you have thorns that protect you from those who do not deserve your love. But don't let those thorns harden your heart, for you are meant to bloom and flourish in the arms of the right person. Have faith IN YOURSELF. Trust in the journey that the universe has planned for you. And when the right person comes along, you will know it in YOUR HEART AND SOUL. And your love will be like a symphony, a beautiful and harmonious melody that will make your heart sing. So don't give up on love. It is out there, waiting for you. And I have no doubt that you will find it; YOU ARE WORTH THE WAIT.

Something deep within me, something beyond my
heart's core, wants to scream out to you in the silence
of the night. Something is happening, something
beneath the surface of what we can see. There is a
truth bubbling up like the pits of an active volcano.
A fire is beginning within you, and you have no
idea what you'll do with it or how you'll survive this
transformation from within. This isn't the first time
you've felt it, and it won't be the last. There have been
times in your life when the heat you felt growing
scared you, but not tonight, not in this moment.
The hotter it becomes, the stronger your tolerance.
The taller it grows, the more willing you are to let it
out. And when you do, I hope you burn down every
bridge that allowed the wrong people to reach you. I
hope you set fire to every memory that haunts you in
the middle of the night. I hope you find the courage
to be transformed by the fire into the phoenix that
lies dormant within your soul, ready to be awakened
by your desire to find strength after the heartbreak.

I know it hasn't been easy. It's like you're wandering in the dark of your desire to feel loved; you're vulnerable and open, but the ones you've given your heart to have not been capable of matching your emotional effort. I'm asking you not to give up on your idea of love. I'm asking you not to allow your exes the power to dictate your future. I'm asking you to turn that love inward. I'm asking you to give yourself everything you've attempted to find in others because, alone, you have everything you need and more. It's not easy on this journey toward real love, but you are strong enough, even when you second-guess yourself.

Her presence is like a bridge that slowly leads people from trouble to a place of peace and love.

_____

She triumphed over darkness.

———————————————

When she knew what she was worth, she broke free
and flew higher.

_____

When trouble came, she lit a fierce, self-controlled
fire from within.

I hope that, one day, you'll find the strength to walk away so that you can walk closer to yourself with the understanding and realization that you alone have always been everything you needed.

———————————

A woman who has the courage to walk away from a
relationship that causes her heart to hurt discovers
that she is standing on the brink of an infinite
number of possibilities in the vast and limitless
tapestry that is life. As she sets off on a journey, she
is comforted by the gentle whispers of self-love and
comprehension. Along the way, she comes across
a world in which her heart is treasured and her
dreams are tended to. She blossoms like a dazzling
flower, engulfed by the warmth of a love that heals,
uplifts, and inspires her with every stride forward
that she takes, revealing the unexplored beauty of
the potential that lies inside her own being. She
transcends into a realm where her heart is cradled
in the delicate hands of a love that is true, kind, and
enduring with each new horizon that she traverses,
leaving the shadows of her past behind her each time.

Empowered and defiant, she walked away. Her stride screamed, "I will never settle."

———————————————

She danced gracefully through life's storms; she found music in the rain.

_____

Without realizing it, she was building up the courage
to walk away, even in times when she believed she'd
never be able to let go.

———————————————

Someone considerate. Someone selfless. Someone who makes an effort on your behalf. Someone who does not raise the level of tension in the room and someone who does not withhold their attention from you. Someone who prioritizes you above all else. Someone who puts in the same amount of effort as you do, someone who is willing to compete with your level of exertion. You may have imagined that, because you are capable of all of these things, it would be simpler to attract the appropriate person; however, in most cases, this is not the case. It appears as though finding that someone has been one of the most difficult obstacles you have had in your life. And I hope that I have your attention now, and I hope that despite the anguish that you have felt in your heart, you are reading this. I really hope that you are aware that there is still time for you to go to where you should be and to be with someone who values you and appreciates what you bring to the world.

It is critical to cut ties with people who have caused you pain. It's vital to put some distance between yourself and people who don't belong on your journey with you.

There is nothing wrong with being alone, because when you are alone, you are in the best position to discover a greater love of yourself and potentially a connection that pushes you to grow.

It is essential to have a clear understanding of the benefits that come with moving on. When you finally decide to let go of the past and go on with your life, you will uncover everything that was always yours but that you were unable to actually achieve since you were with the wrong person at the time. It's possible that I'm speaking to the person who requires this the most; perhaps you are the person I've been thinking about and writing about the whole time.

There is a genuine love waiting for you somewhere in the world, and you shouldn't make do with someone who doesn't fully represent what you believe you should have in a partner.

She was forged in the fire of life's challenges, and yet she remained soft like petals but unbreakable like steel.

With dignity and poise, she bears the burden of the world, and even in the midst of chaos, she shines a guiding light of love and hope for those around her.

―――――――――――――――――――

She lay in bed, staring at the ceiling, muttering to herself, "It eventually gets better," and repeating the phrase like a mantra while she went through the motions of doing so. She had no idea how or when it would occur, but she tried everything in her power to cling to the tiniest shred of hope she could find. After that, she awoke one morning to find that the burden that had been sitting on her chest had been lifted, just as she had been promised. Even though the pain was still present, it had become duller and was easier to deal with. She was well aware that she still had a long journey in front of her, but for the first time in a while, she got the sense that she was up to the challenge. She comforted herself by telling herself, "It eventually gets better," finding solace in the straightforward yet profound reality of those words.

i long for you
like miles on highways
or the shoreline beside the sea

waiting patiently
for you to decide
that you're ready
to long for me

_____

I write about you, but words can never do you any justice, for your existence is too profound for the lines that make up these letters. And still I write in hopes that when these books are made available to the world that you will get your hands on one, and maybe, just maybe, I can get my hands on your heart.

_____

There was something incredible in her eyes, something stained into her memory. Love was always a dream, but at this moment, she'd discovered a new romance as she stared into the mirror to find her reflection.

———————————————

Women like you are not made for mediocre claims of love. Women like you are not made to accept empty promises and weak apologies. Women like you are not made to be overlooked and unappreciated. Women like you are not to be forgotten. Women like you burn through doubt; women like you move mountains. Women such as yourself can walk through flames and quicksand. Women like you are rare and should never settle for anything that feels ordinary or, at the very least, anything that makes you feel less than who you already are.

———————————————

I know that there's this thing within your heart, a
secret you've yet to tell. You lose sleep over it; most
nights, you lie there, restless, with a scream of truth
trapped in your throat. You're not trying to mislead
others with your smile; that display of joy is just an
attempt to remain strong under the circumstances. I
know that you are tired of waiting for the opportunity
to bare your soul; I can feel the ache in your heart as
you read these words. It's almost as if you feel my eyes
looking into the windows of your anguish, or maybe
you don't feel as alone as you did before picking
up this book. Regardless of what you feel in this
moment, I just want you to feel seen. I want you to
know that your journey matters and that, no matter
how sad it gets, no matter how rough it becomes, you
are fully equipped with everything you need in order
to get through this.

She's tired of apologies without any change in action.

———————————————

She's tired of pretty words and empty promises.

———————————

She's tired of being asked to compromise her peace of mind for your drama and toxic behavior.

She's tired of feeling like she has to apologize when she's done nothing wrong.

_____

She's tired of feeling like she's being punished when all she wants is to be loved in a way that makes her feel secure.

———————————

She's tired of wasting her energy and time in a relationship that isn't meant to go in the right direction.

She's tired, and she knows that leaving you will grant her the rest that she deserves and the opportunity to find something better.

———————————

A MIDNIGHT MOON

a brief screenplay by **r.h. Sin**

INT. LIVING ROOM—Night

> **(She sits on the couch, a packed suitcase beside her. Her soon-to-be ex-boyfriend stands in front of her, confused at what he's seeing.)**

Him: "What's going on? Please, don't do this. We can work through it."

Her: "No, I'm not falling for this again. We can't. We've been trying to work through this for too long, and it's not getting any better. It's almost like I see what you could be, I see your potential, but who you've chosen to be, it's just too far of a wait for who you need to be in order for me to stay."

Him: "You're not supposed to give up on the ones you love . . . I love you. Don't you love me anymore?"

Her: "Love isn't enough. It's not enough to make up for all the times you've hurt me. All the times you've made me feel like I'm not enough. In the beginning, when I fell, I thought at the very least you would fall beside me, but one morning, I woke up to your absence not only physically but emotionally. This idea of Love, this room of Love, had always been a place made for one. Always occupied by me."

Him: "I'll change. I promise. Just give me another chance."

Her: "I've given you so many chances. In fact, I almost tricked myself into believing that my trying harder would somehow make you want to choose me. And, every time, you've let me down. I can't keep doing this to myself."

Him: "Please. Think about all the good times we've had. Don't throw it all away."

3

Her: "I'm not throwing anything away. In fact, I cherished every bit of what we cultivated, and so I have no regrets. I'm choosing to love myself more than I love you. I'm choosing to walk in love, and that also means walking away from you. I deserve to feel supported and loved for all that I am, and that's not something I'm willing to compromise on anymore."

Him: "I don't understand. What did I do wrong?"

Her: "It's not just one thing. This pain I've felt is the making of the many moments I longed to be chosen but often went overlooked. It's the way you talk to me. It's the way you treat me. It's the way you make me feel about myself. I deserve better than that, and it took me some time to understand this, but now there's no going back."

Him: "I'll do anything to make it right. Just tell me what to do."

Her: "It's not about what you can do. It's about who you are. And, right now, you're not the person I need in my life."

Him: "So that's it? You're just going to leave me?"

Her: "I'm not leaving you, Mike. I'm leaving the person you've become. And I'm doing it for myself."

(He looks at her, tears in his eyes.)

Him: "I'll always love you. I can't believe this is happening right now."

Her: "And I'll always love the person you could've been. But I can't keep holding on to that person. It's time for me to move on."

4

(She stands up, picks up her suitcase,
and heads toward the door.)

Him: "Where are you going?"

Her: "I'm going to start a new chapter of my life.
One that doesn't include the hurtful words, ideas,
and moments you helped me write."

(She opens the door and turns to
look at him one last time.)

Her: "When I was all in, you rarely gave or matched
my effort. When I was fully here, you were nowhere
to be found. My heart used to be a song in the keys
of your name, but then that song became a melody of
sadness. Love should be beautiful; Love is a garden;
my Love was a garden, and you failed to nurture the
roots. You treated me like weeds as if you had no
idea that I was a beautiful and strong flower waiting
to bloom. Goodbye."

(She walks out the door to greet a midnight moon,
leaving him alone in the living room, tears streaming
down his face and a pit in his chest deep enough to
hold all of the regret he'll accumulate with time.)

END SCENE